BLACK DIAMONDS

By Daphne A. Kennedy-Johnson

ILLUSTRATED BY **Derrell Spicy**   GRAPHIC LAYOUT BY **Carolyn Zomphier**   EDITED BY **Jeffrey S. Johnson**

Published by Sibling Thrivalry, LLC

www.siblingthrivalry.com
ISBN# 978-0-9789334-2-5

Collections

Sibling Thrivalry, LLC was created to provide products that build self esteem, encourage collaborative play and strengthen sibling relationships. Thrivalry is our term for the positive change that occurs when loved ones transcend rivalry and develop thriving relationships.

BOOKS

Brothers Are Forever Friends

In good times and bad, brothers are lifetime friends! Disagreements and different abilities do not destroy a brother's love.

The Power of a Baby Girl

It's a girl! A family learns that a baby girl brings the power of love! The baby of the bunch knows her special place in the family from the very beginning.

GAME

Sibling College

Sibling College is a "getting to know you" family game. The game inspires family bonding. It is great for reunions and parties, and is great for travel! Everyone wins when all players demonstrate knowledge of each other.

To find out more about **Sibling Thrivalry, LLC** visit us at
www.siblingthrivalry.com

Sibling Thrivalry, LLC
3011 W. 183rd St. #266
Homewood, IL 60430

For the Black Diamonds in my life

**My mother Alice,
My daughter Destiny and
My nieces Cydnee and Alicia**

*Always know that you are
rare and precious!*

Momma and Daddy, you say that I'm beautiful.
You tell me this all the time!
It's difficult to accept,
When others criticize these looks of mine.
I think you have a biased opinion.
You will always tell me that everything is fine!

Big sister doesn't look like me at all!
She doesn't get the same teasing.
Sometimes I get jealous and wish that I looked like her.
I wish my looks were more pleasing!

Even grown women worry about
Lips being too small or too full,
Or their noses being too broad or too keen.

They've had lifetimes of too much feedback
That was too spiteful, too ignorant or too mean!

Even grown women worry about being
Too hippy, too voluptuous, too angular, too flat,

Too skinny, or too fat!

Yet we come in all different sizes,
And there is beauty in them all!
Who wants a mosaic
With the same colors and shapes
To adorn and beautify our walls?

There will always be someone who loves your look
And recognizes you for the queen that you are!
There will always be someone who wants to copy your look.
You don't have to look very far.

Too curvy, too lean,
Too dark, too light,
Too short, too tall-
People will comment about it all!

I couldn't help but overhear what you're saying, little sis.
I did not realize your concerns before!
People go out of their way to point out my flaws.
I'm under scrutiny even more!

They tell you that you are too dark.
Among other things, they tell me that I am too light.
I think that if I looked like you, I would be just right!

As diversely colored as a rainbow,
Black has many shades.
God has the ultimate paint brush.
You are beautiful queens that God has made!

I want both of you girls to color me a picture.

We're too old for that!

You are only allowed to use one crayon...
They'll be dull pictures, and that's a fact!

If you get my point, then I guess you don't have to do the picture,
But a drawing is nothing without a beautiful mixture
Of color . . .dark and light colors alike!
If you think for a moment, you'll realize that I'm right!

Some say that it's "pleasing to be plump,"
Others say that it's "in to be thin."
Society's ideals go in and out of fashion, and really,
We can look at this now and know that it seems silly!

Popular standards of beauty change all the time,
But as time has shown
When you look at an old picture you can see classic beauty,
Although the fad of the time is unknown.

You are not a fad, you are not a trend.
Fads and trends have their moments,
Then come to an end.

You are a classic.
You will never go "out of style."
Nothing is as timeless
As your beautiful smiles!

There is a huge industry that is getting rich
From liposuctions and other reductions,
Padded clothing and augmentation,
Draining the confidence of an entire nation!

COOKIE
CUTTER
PACKAGE
1/2 OFF

While you are trying to be like someone else,
Someone else is surely trying to be like you.

Bigger is better...smaller is better...
The industry sees that both of these must be true!

Since I am beautiful on the outside
And I know I am beautiful on the inside,
The viewer's perspective is where the problem must lie!

I guess it's true… the very things about my looks
That supposedly make me less than ideal
Are making someone a profit!
My style does have appeal!

Creams to lighten skin,
Tans to darken skin,
Weaves of bone straight hair,
Weaves of kinky hair-

Dark skin, light skin, straight hair, kinky hair-
So beautiful are these extremes!
Let's not forget,
Beautiful also is everything in between!

All three of you are MY diamonds!

Black diamonds are not all the same shade.
They come in different colors.
They are rare and unique,
Standing out from the others!

Diamonds come in carats,
Which describe their weights.
Some prefer small diamond clusters,
Some prefer large solitaire shapes.

Diamonds come in many cuts, including
The round shape and the pear,
Along with the emerald, a rectangular shape and
The princess shape, a square.

The diamond does not yell "pick me, pick me!"
It sits and shines quietly.
It is selected by the most deserving one,
Who knows its charm is second to none!

The untrained eye can look at a diamond and see glass,
Yet the diamond is not any less appealing.
I'm glad that we're having this discussion!
We need to deal with your insecure feelings.

All human diamonds are complete with flaws and beauty.
Some are difficult to see with the naked eye.
Make sure that you don't sell yourself short.
Retain your beauty that is inside!

Like the black diamond, in society's view,
Different always ascends from "deficient" to desired.
Don't let inconsiderate words demoralize you.
Heed my words and be inspired!

The young woman must have clarity,
Because it is her right from birth
To filter through her self-perceived flaws
And have a good sense of self worth.

Repeat after me!

"My worth is not limited to
How others view my shine.
I know that I sparkle, AND
Inner beauty is mine!"

Momma and Daddy,
You're pretty convincing!
I have to admit, I look really good!
I look the way that God intended.
I look just the way that I should!

I'm feeling much better, you've removed my doubts.
I'm happy that you took the time.
You are right, I am pretty fabulous!
I'm what you "old school" folks call fine!

Baby girl, I am proud
that you're beautiful!

My sister, I am proud
that you're beautiful, too!

About the Author

Daphne Kennedy-Johnson has a Master's Degree in finance and is a Certified Public Accountant. She is a stay at home mom. This is her third book.

Mrs. Johnson established Sibling Thrivalry, LLC to create books and games that help to strengthen sibling relationships, foster self esteem and encourage collaborative play.

Mrs. Johnson's hobbies are genealogy and track and field. She lives in the Chicago area with her husband Jeff, sons Jeffrey and Julian, and daughter Destiny.